Visible Time:
The Work of David Claerbout

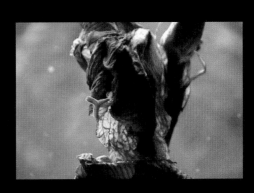

Visible Time:
The Work of David Claerbout

Essays by Joanna Lowry, David Green and Gregory Currie
Edited by David Green

photoWORKS

Four Persons Standing, 1999.
Video Installation, b/w, sound.
Installation view at De
Vereniging SMAK Stedelijk
Museum voor Actuelle Kunst,
Gent, 1999.

A man and a girl sit at a table, framed by the roof and wall of a loggia. It could be a private holiday house: white concrete and modernist in style; its stark walls and pillars both frame and bisect the space, inscribing a formalist field of abstract relationships. The sun spills over the building but the couple are sitting half in the shadows. They are quite still; the young girl is drawing. It is a scene of total absorption. I am gazing at the scene from another world and it seems, within the artificial frame provided by the white beams of the building, to be totally contained and complete. As I move closer the girl looks up, turns her head to look at me, then drops her head and returns to her task. It is the smallest of incidents – a movement that indicates the subtlest of changes in the spatial configuration of people and place; a movement that barely indicates, in the way in which it pierces the stillness of the moment, an experience of time. Something has happened. And it didn't just happen in the picture. It happened to me.

Why does this momentary encounter transfix me? Why does this, the briefest of incidents, seem so pregnant with significance? What is this strange sense of metaphysical truth that floods over me as my eyes meet hers? As that gaze reaches out from within the frame of the picture and acknowledges my presence, or at least the presence of a spectator. That turn of the head, of course, seems so charged simply because it effects a shift between two completely different optical regimes – the one, contained within the frame, absorbed, an object of contemplation that is complete and autonomous: a world that holds the spectator at a distance – perhaps in a position of optical mastery – but nevertheless far away. The other regime is inclusive, engaged, dynamic; the spectator is no longer a theoretical personality – it is you or I – and we are called into a dialogic relationship with the girl in the picture, and for one brief moment we become active players in a theatrical space that includes our own spatiality, our own sense of time.[1]

Central to our concerns here is the way in which the transition between one type of attention and another is registered by an 'event'. This small incident – a girl turning her head – is significant because it is a marker of this transition; it can be thought of as a sort of hinge opening a door between these two types of visual contract with the image. And in this sense it is, I would argue, a very distinctive kind of sign, monitoring the boundaries of the image whilst simultaneously breaching them. The event thus introduces a shift in the way we view the work, and in that sense it can be seen to be performative. It also, in producing this shift in the terms of our engagement with the image, exposes the way in which these boundaries – which seem at first to be ones that pertain to the aesthetics of the image – are also deeply entwined with our modern sense of the relationship between time and space. What is thrown into a kind of uncertainty is the terms of our relationship to the image and to the scene depicted there, a scene that seems, in its meticulous formalism, to represent some quintessential melancholic essence of modern life.

The event, as I have described it here, has emerged in critical discourse as one of the key terms in the analysis of modernity. It has been characterised by a number of writers and theorists in ways that position it as symptomatic of the cultural and technological changes that have characterised modernity: as a phenomenon that achieves a kind of cultural prominence because of the changes in the ways in which we experience time and space in contemporary post-industrial society. The writings of theorists of the postmodern condition such as Lyotard, Jameson, Crary, Virilio and Kwinter,[2] have all contributed further to our understanding of contemporary experience as essentially fragmented and disjunctive. The impact of technology upon the dismantling of a classical understanding of space and time and its gradual replacement by a phenomenology of indeterminacy and chance has become almost a cliché and has contributed to a new orthodoxy whereby the collapse of the grand modernist historical narrative is replaced by a plurality of postmodern ahistorical events.

But the growing significance of the event also can be seen as a phenomenon whose emergence is deeply intertwined with the developing histories of photographic and cinematic technologies. If these are technologies that stop, capture, record and reproduce time, and that actively intervene, through their representational functions, in our cultural understanding of time, then they have also contributed fundamentally to the way in which we understand the very concept of the event as a kind of sign, as a sign that is defined through its relationship to contingency and trauma.

Perhaps the most influential writer on the nature of modernity, Walter Benjamin, drew our attention to the event through his description of the shocks and traumas that permeated the everyday experience of the modern subject. His characterisation through an analysis of the writings of Baudelaire of the man in the street who is assailed and buffeted by strangers, experiences and encounters over which he has no control, and is subject fundamentally to contingency and chance, has dominated the discussion of modernity for the last half a century. Alongside this he developed of course possibly the most significant theorisation of the impact of photographic technologies in his two essays 'A Short History of Photography' and 'The Work of Art in the Age of Mechanical Reproduction'. Central to his analysis of the technologies of photography and cinema in these essays was the sense that they were, in effect, traumatic. The capacity of these technologies to disrupt the temporal and cut into the stream of events, surgically penetrating our experience, was at the heart of his arguments. The event as a trauma was, in effect, a consequence of this dividing and rupturing of experience by technology. Through the prism of Benjamin's writings contingency and trauma can be seen as twinned concepts reflecting not only the social experience of modernity but also being fundamental to the technologies of representation that have emerged within it.[3]

What Benjamin also drew our attention towards was the fact that the invention of photography changed our relationship to time – and not through representing it as a painter might – but through producing it. Photographic technologies actively produced new means of experiencing and conceptualising time. His description of early portrait photographs of the mid-nineteenth century that had been taken with necessarily long exposures reflects upon the way they produce in us, through the very fact of having been taken, an experience of an expanded and uncanny temporality. It is indeed the attempt to understand the effect of this experience of a displaced temporality that has dominated writing about photography. Both photography and cinema, and nowadays we must include also video and the digital interface, are technologies that have

1 My analysis here is indebted to the analysis of eighteenth century history painting by Michael Fried in *Absorption and Theatricality: Painting and Beholder in the Age of Diderot*, University of California Press, 1980. See also my own essay 'Within the Horizon of Time' in *Rineke Dijkstra: Location*, The Photographers' Gallery, 1997.

2 Jean-François Lyotard, *The Postmodern Condition: a report on knowledge*, Manchester University Press, 1984; Fredric Jameson, *Postmodernism, The Cultural Logic of Late Capitalism*, Verso 1991; Jonathan Crary, *Suspensions of Perception: Attention, spectacle and modern culture*, MIT Press 1999; Paul Virilio, *The Vision Machine*, BFI, 1994; Sanford Kwinter, *Architectures of Time: Towards a Theory of the Event in Modernist Culture*, MIT Press, 2002.

3 Walter Benjamin 'The Work Of Art in the Age of Mechanical Reproduction' in *Illuminations* ed. Hannah Arendt, Schocken Books, New York, 1969; also, for a discussion of trauma, contingency and the photographic image, see Ulrich Baer *Spectral Evidence*, MIT Press, 2002.

Untitled (Carl and Julie), 2000.
Interactive Video Installation,
b/w, silent.
Previous page: Installation view
at INOVA Institute of Visual Arts,
Milwaukee WI, 2001.

expanded the language of temporality. Both the still and the moving image are phenomena that have produced new forms of experience of presentness, instantaneity, duration, and repetition. They have shown us how time can be stopped, extended, folded and cut. But in doing this, and in thus providing us with the armature for the creation of an essentially modern cultural language of time, they have implicitly sutured themselves into the historical emergence of the concept of the event.[4]

The still photograph, in its isolation of a moment of time, constitutes an exemplar of the most minimal event – and yet through its very existence as an image that contains no time it, in an important sense, denies the very possibility of the event. Poised between the before and the after, the what-has-been and the what-will-be, it is the framing of the possibility of nothing happening at all. The event itself is that which brought the image into being: it is displaced and can be understood better as the act of taking the photograph, the click of the shutter. Indeed photography is revealed as essentially performative. Similarly if we turn to film, Mary Ann Doane, in a recent analysis of early cinema, has commented upon the way in which the problem of the boundary of the event constituted a fundamental problem for film-makers – a problem that seemed to be not so much pragmatic as ontological: in recording something on film how might one determine where to begin and where to end? Was the event itself defined in the realm of the real, the pro-filmic, or through the logic of the film itself? She argues that the fundamental indeterminacy of this problematic suggests a complicity between the technology and the event that underpinned a shift toward a distinctively modern concept of time.[5]

What is common to the technologies of photography and film here is their dependence upon the mechanicity of the image and its consequent contingency. They both produce images that are framed by mechanical intervention rather than by symbolic operation and the events that they bring into being are thus pervaded by contingency and chance. When Benjamin coined the term 'the optical unconscious' to describe this disquieting and revelatory potential within the photographic image he was revealing in his choice of terminology the power of our desire for there to be some structure and meaning to this potentially overwhelming arbitrariness of the world.

In a sense the event – the something happening – is central to all of David Claerbout's work, but always as something that emerges out of this kind of rupturing of a visual regime; a moment that exposes some of the seams that hold our modern sense of time and space together.[6] Claerbout's work thus always addresses the spectator as a 'modern subject' poised in a position of indeterminacy in relationship to the image, negotiating a number of different relationships to the boundaries of the frame, and in a position of self-awareness about his or her position at the intersection of the technologies of space and time – photographic, filmic, digital. In this sense, then, the event, as a phenomenon produced through these technologies, also contributes to the continuing debate around the concerns of modernist aesthetics and their impact upon experimental film and installation practices. This debate, emerging out of the influential critique of minimalism by American critic Michael Fried and later countered by the influence of Rosalind Krauss, has underpinned many of the discussions about ways in which technologically-based forms of art practice, experimental film, video, expanded cinema, can be said to orient themselves around notions of the 'medium' and of an ambivalent relationship to the spectator.[7]

The event, therefore, is crucial in Claerbout's work as a device that, in its manipulation of temporal technologies, positions the spectator in an ambivalent and uncertain relationship to the image. But the event always takes place within a carefully framed tableau – and one recurring feature in his work is the dependence of that tableau upon the spaces of architecture. The very size of the projection pieces, which are often designed to fill the space of an actual wall or to bisect a space like an architectural partition, invite us to perceive an analogy between the screen and the building itself – with all of the ambivalence about the position of the embodied spectator in relationship to that building/screen that such an analogy suggests. In many of his works Claerbout situates the event in a formal relationship to the representation of architecture and through this to the idea of modernity as defined through a spatial aesthetic. The architectural presence of the holiday house in *Untitled (Carl and Julie)* is totally dominating; Claerbout uses it as a powerful framing device to establish a theatrical space for his two actors, with the architecture indicating a kind of framing device

For a discussion of Claerbout's work in relationship to a Deleuzian concept of time see my essay 'Slowing Down', *Portfolio Magazine*, June 2003.

5 Mary Ann Doane, *The Emergence of Cinematic Time: Modernity, Contingency and the Archive*, Harvard University Press, 2002. Doane provides an extended analysis of the importance of the concept of the 'event' in early cinema

6 The concept of 'something happening' refers to Lyotard's analysis of the relationship between the event and the sublime in 'The Sublime and the Avant-Garde' *The Lyotard Reader*, ed. Andrew Benjamin, Basil Blackwell, 1989.

or threshold, but he also uses it as a way of situating them within an abstract visual field that positions the image within an optically defined modernist aesthetic. Finally, and perhaps most importantly, we experience the architecture itself as the signifier of a peculiarly modern inhabitation of space – and in this sense as something that implies that these works have something to do with the impact of history, with the nature of modern life.

Architecture is a dominant presence in a number of Claerbout's other works. In *Man Under Arches* the projected image depicts a frontal view of two industrial arches. A character is standing in the dark shadows behind them. As the visitor enters the room a sensor is triggered and the figure slips around the corner of a building and disappears from sight. When the visitor leaves the room the figure returns. He is always elusive, always just not seen. It is clear from this description the extent to which, in this installation, Claerbout has selected once again the most minimal and incidental of events – the triggering of a missed encounter, the replaying of a frustrated desire. If *Untitled (Carl and Julie)* presented us with a moment of interactivity that fractures the boundaries of the image through a gaze that looks out at us, this installation does the reverse: standing in front of the image our desire is projected onto this elusive figure who draws it through the image into a space behind it, out of sight. In each case Claerbout is using the device of the event to trouble the tableau that appears on the screen, to indicate a space of the medium that has a three dimensional psychological depth that includes the spectator. It is a space in which the architecture plays a dual role – both framing the image and reinforcing the perimeters of the projection – and also offering us a spatial language that goes beyond the surface of the screen. Installed as a large screen projection this, like a number of Claerbout's other works, invokes a bodily response from the spectator – nearly life-size they operate as near simulacra of the spaces they represent. The archways, their flatness almost palpable in the cool refined light, offer a threshold through which we enter into a dark and uncanny space.

This subtle parallel drawn between the surface of the screen and the space of architecture is a recurrent theme in Claerbout's work, and the events that he records (or 'produces') are often designed to draw our attention to this complicity between the two forms. In many cases it is the event that allows us to breach the frame of the work and occupy a place within the projected space. For instance in *The Rocking Chair* a woman is rocking quietly back and forth in her rocking chair on a porch, a dark doorway behind her offering the suggestion of an interior space. The rocking motion has the interminable regularity of a clock, of mechanical repetition, of a video loop. When we enter the room we create a disturbance: the rocking stops, the woman raises her head as though to register the interruption – and then resumes her rocking. The scene is projected onto a large screen suspended in the middle of the gallery so that we are invited to walk around it. On this side of the screen we discover that we are now positioned as though inside the house, looking past the woman out into the sunlight beyond. We are now standing in the uncanny darkness behind the image. The hidden interior is 'behind' the screen we first encountered and there is something distinctly strange about our occupation of that imaginary place. In this piece the identification of the doorway of the building with the screen onto which it is projected is explicitly worked through. Both of them are presented as a kind of threshold that we must pass through, from the light into the dark and back again.

The subtlety of the relationship between the dark spaces created by the buildings in his images and the surface of the screen is captured in *Four Persons Standing* where the surface of the image is brought into a kind of tension with the dark space beyond. Two men and two women stand on a pavement in front of a building. The two men are looking at one of the women. She is distinguished by her light coat, which contrasts with three other besuited figures. The dynamics between the four figures are framed by the criss-crossing structure of beams and columns within the space. Over a period of time the light grows and fades, creating subtly different effects upon our reading of the image. This encounter – unexplained and without incident – continually threatens to disappear into the dark depths of the building behind.

In an essay entitled 'Dark Space' Anthony Vidler describes a design for a 'Temple of Death' by the eighteenth century architect Boullée.[8] Inspired by the experience of seeing his own shadow cast by the moonlight onto the forest floor, Boullée conceived of a building which would itself be a reminder of the relationship between light and shade: a horizontal shallow facade, stripped of decoration, subtended by the deep shadows that represent our mortality.

7 Michael Fried 'Art and Objecthood' in *Minimal Art, A Critical Anthology*, New York, Dutton, 1968; Rosalind Krauss *'A Voyage on the North Sea': Art in the Age of the Post-Medium Condition*, Thames and Hudson, 1999.

8 Anthony Vidler, *The Architectural Uncanny, Essays in the Modern Unhomely*, MIT Press, 1994 pp 167 – 177.

would be, according to Boullée, a 'buried architecture forming by means of materials absorbent to light, the black picture of an architecture of shadows depicted by the effect of even blacker shadows'. This building, which in a special sense seemed to embody the shadow of the figure of the architect himself, was what Vidler describes as 'a virtual architecture of negativity'. And Vidler goes on to discuss the place of this imaginary building within the context of an Enlightenment discourse of visibility, light and knowledge, arguing that the emergence of such a set of precepts was necessarily paralleled by their mirror image in a spatial phenomenology of darkness. In constructing this building out of the shadows, he argues, Boullée was creating a self-conscious architecture of the uncanny:

'For by flattening his shadow, so to speak, on the surface of a building that was itself nothing but (negative) surface, Boullée had created an image of an architecture not only without real depth, but one that deliberately played on the ambiguities between flatness and infinite depth, between his own shadow and the void. The building as the double of the death of the subject, translated this disappearance into experienced spatial uncertainty.'[9]

In describing an architecture that was, as it were, the negative of blackness, an architecture that hovered between the concept of a depthless facade and the intolerable void of dark space, Boullée was perhaps prefiguring the imaginary space of architecture created by photography. For in the photograph the uncanny doubling of space emerges out of the chemical dialectic of light and dark; the illusory screen of the photographic surface rising, like Boullée's facade, out of the darkroom itself. But if the dark space of Boullée's eighteenth century imagination was situated in the gothic imagery of stone walls, dungeons and burial chambers, the dark architectural spaces of photography today are located in the spaces of the unconscious, spaces which, moreover, are delineated by the technological process itself.

Claerbout's video-projection piece Untitled (single channel view) explores this intersection between the architectural and the photographic in a different way. The scene is the interior of a classroom in a boy's school. This room is a quintessentially modern institutional space – clear unadorned lines and surfaces, a brutalist brick wall. The tops of the desks are empty, their surfaces

flecting the light that streams in on them from the gleaming white mono-chrome of the window that extends across one wall. The boys seated at their desks appear to be about twelve years old – some of them are looking towards the window – it feels as though something is about to happen. But nothing does happen. It is quite still – except for the shadow thrown onto the back wall of two trees, their leaves moving in the wind.

In this installation the event is signified not by the triggering of a movement – but by the stopping of it. The impact of the stilled image is accentuated by the contrast with the softly moving trees outside. The juxtaposition of two technologies of time once again creates a kind of internal horizon of the event. But more importantly Claerbout presents us with two forms of image in production: the shadow of the moving trees cast on the wall presents us with one kind of screen – a metaphor for cinema; this is contrasted with the transfixed figures of the boys, who appear themselves to be almost 'being developed' by the light flooding in from the window in a classroom that has been transformed into a giant pinhole camera. The image suggests a modernist interpretation of Plato's cave, whose inhabitants are chained inside, able to see the outside world only through the medium of shadows thrown upon the wall. But it also offers a complex meditation upon the relationships between the technologies of film, photography and architecture. The horizon of the event – at the seam between the stillness of photography and the movement of film – is projected onto the space of the classroom producing a melancholic allegory of modernity.

The juxtaposition here of a set of arguments about the manipulation of photographic and filmic technologies with a set of arguments about architecture and space is not arbitrary. Contemporary theorists of modernity have been preoccupied by the impact on modern consciousness of both photographic technologies and of architectures. The argument that the modern subject is inscribed within a peculiarly modern sense of space and time has become almost a cliché of contemporary thought. Claerbout is also not alone amongst contemporary artists in his attempt to find, through a conflation of the filmic and the architectural, a visual form that will allow the relationship between these aspects of modern experience to be revealed. Artists like Tacita Dean, who surveys a reconstructed Berlin through the moving windows of a revolving restaurant,[10] or Sam Taylor Wood who creates panoramic narratives that scan a room in five seconds and through three hundred and sixty degrees, or Jane and Louise Wilson who take us on elaborate multi-screened tours of the Houses of Parliament, deserted military bases and nuclear sites, have all created works which build upon the structural affinities between architecture and film. And in all of those works there is an ambiguity created through the way in which the work simultaneously addresses both the spectator of the film and the embodied inhabitant of the space of the buildings being filmed.

The modern building thus emerges as a kind of melancholic motif, whose identity is locked into a history of film – a history that can be traced back to Lumière's factory gates opening and closing to allow the workers to go home: the film rolling, the projector running, the gates framing the event.

10 A suggestive discussion of Tacita Dean's representation of modern architecture and its relationship to film can be found in Tamara Trodd, 'Film at the End of the Twentieth Century: Obsolescence and the Medium in the Work of Tacita Dean' Object, no. 6, University College London,

Rocking Chair, 2003.
Interactive Video Installation
b/w, silent

Nightscape Lightbox (second),
2002-2003. 125 x 146 x 20 cm

Nightscape Lightbox (fourth),
2002-2003. 125 x 146 x 20 cm

Nightscape Lightbox (first),
2002-2003. 125 x 146 x 20 cm

Nightscape Lightbox (fifth),
2002-2003. 125 x 146 x 20 cm

The Visibility of Time

In David Claerbout's large scale video projection *Vietnam, 1967, near Duc Pho*, the disintegrating body of a American fighter plane shot down by 'friendly fire' is caught suspended above a verdant undulating landscape, the contours of which are made evident by the shadows of clouds that roll gently and endlessly across its surface. Whilst the fragments of the plane remain frozen in space and time, traceable to the momentary opening of a photographic shutter nearly four decades ago, the landscape against which they are set, filmed more recently, is caught in that state of an unfolding present tense that belongs to the moving image.[1] To an audience who are well accustomed to a plethora of visual effects made possible by electronic and digital technologies and widely employed by the various armatures of the culture industry to create virtual worlds, this impossible conjuncture of the different spatio-temporal relationships of the still and moving image fashioned here by Claerbout should hardly surprise us. But it does. Despite, or perhaps because of, its evident lack of spectacularity, *Vietnam, 1967, near Duc Pho*, is deeply fascinating. It holds our attention, I believe, through our inability to reconcile our understanding and expectations concerning the differences between photography and film, differences which ultimately have been thought to lie within the distinct ontologies of the still and moving image.[2]

To approach Claerbout's work in this way is to summon up ways of thinking about different artistic mediums in terms of their 'specificity'; about what fundamental characteristics or properties are seen to define a given medium and, at the same time, to distinguish it from other mediums. However, whilst I will use the notion of medium specificity to discuss Claerbout's work I want to do so without recourse to a form of essentialism that has undermined its credibility in the domains of both art history and film theory. Rather than the notion that

---

1 This work was based on a photograph taken by the Japanese photographer Hiromichi Mine, a year before he died. David Claerbout returned in 2000 to the place at which the original photograph was taken. Positioning himself as close as possible to the point from which Mine's image taken, he proceeded to take at regular intervals numerous digital photographs. These have been morphed by a computer programme to produce a 'moving image'. The full title of the work is *Vietnam, 1967, near Duc Pho (reconstruction after Hiromichi Mine 'Friendly Fire')*.

2 It may seem strange in an essay that argues the case of a notion of medium specificity that I use the term 'film' to refer to works by David Claerbout that are either video-based or which use digital technology to produce animated, moving images. Whilst I recognize the necessity to ultimately make distinctions between these various ways of producing the 'moving image', which is my primary concern here, the nomenclature of 'film' is adopted for reasons of convenience and convention.

Vietnam, 1967, near Duc Pho (Reconstruction after Hiromishi Mine), 2001. Video Installation, colour, silent. Previous page: Installation view at CGAC Centro Galego de Arte Contemporánea, Santiago de Compostela, 2003.

each medium possesses unique features that are intrinsic, immutable and timeless, features that give it a singular identity, the argument presented here assumes that any medium remains open to change according to varying historical conditions. It seems obvious that a medium can evolve 'internally' by virtue of technological developments that directly affect the nature of its material and physical support. But equally as important is the fact that a medium might be affected by factors external to it: for example, the medium of painting was transformed by the invention of photography. This highlights the fact that not only is a medium defined by historically relative and shifting *perceptions* of what it 'is' but also it is the perceptions of the *differences* between one medium and another which might ultimately prove most important.

In the case of *Vietnam, 1967, near Duc Pho* what I think needs to be resisted is the temptation to regard such a work as exemplifying the ways in which electronic media and digital imaging have been seen as eroding the boundaries between mediums leading to a fusion of forms and novel types of hybridity. The effect of the work itself is indeed quite contrary to this. What one actually experiences or indeed what one sees in this work is not the conflation of photography and film but a conjuncture of the two mediums in which neither ever loses its specificity. We are thus faced with a phenomenon in which two different mediums co-exist and seem to simultaneously occupy the same object. The projection screen here provides a point of intersection for both the photographic and filmic image.

The effect is that, far from the negation of the idea of media specificity, Claerbout's work opens it out for further exploration. In particular, what the work allows or perhaps invites the viewer to do is to reflect upon what we understand to be the features that define one medium in terms of those features that define another. In other words, what *Vietnam, 1967, near Duc Pho* does is to offer the possibility of critically engaging the photograph through film, and not merely in contradistinction with film. At the same time the work opens out film to an analysis made available by photography. I think that the possibility of imagining photography through film and vice versa (with all the implications that this brings in its wake) lies at the heart of much of Claerbout's work to date. But in order to understand what is at stake in this it is necessary to say something of the

ways in which – both historically and philosophically – photography and film have been closely intertwined.

If it has often been taken for granted that the historical emergence of film was originally dependent upon the existence of technologies derived directly from photography, the philosophical bonds between the two medium have assumed no less an orthodoxy in the realms of film theory. Significantly, the very first chapter of André Bazin's classic text *What is Cinema?* is entitled 'The Ontology of the Photographic Image' and the quest to define film by many other writers since has taken the same starting point. Bazin's essay eloquently synthesizes a now familiar perspective on photography that privileges its indexical character and its power to summon up the real by virtue of its mechanical nature. Yet photography's 'realism' is one that assumes a particular spatio-temporal character, one which Bazin implies through opening his essay with reference to the origins of the visual arts in the primitive 'practice of embalming the dead', arresting the passage of time: 'the preservation of life by a representation of life'.[3] It was left, of course, to Roland Barthes to draw out the full implications of the radically different kind of temporality that the photograph brings in its wake.[4] For Barthes the photograph was a unique historical and ontological phenomenon. Its singularity lay with an entirely originary phenomenology of space and time in which the photograph gives rise to the contradictory sense of what is photographed as being both spatially proximate yet temporally distant. The peculiar and paradoxical articulation of space and time that Barthes identifies with the photograph was also evident to some of the earliest commentators on the new medium but it seems possible that it is only with the later advent of film that the discussion of photography comes to be dominated by the concept of time. Moreover what happens when photography and film come to be compared is that something of the spatio-temporal ambivalence that Barthes sees as endemic to the photographic image is lost in favour of an almost exclusive preoccupation with the photograph as marking a moment that is firmly and irretrievably located in the past.

Seizing on Barthes' notion that the photograph can never testify to the presence of its referent but only to the fact of its 'having been there', Christian Metz has argued that the prevailing sense with film is 'there it is'. And the sole

3 See André Bazin 'The Ontology of Photography' in Peninah R. Petruch (ed) *The Camera Viewed: Writings on Twentieth-Century Photography, Vol. 2,* Dutton Paperback, New York, n.d.

4 The key early essay by Barthes is 'The Rhetoric of the Image' in *Image, Music, Text*, ed. Stephen Heath, Fontana, 1977. In the same volume two other essays, 'The Third Meaning' and 'Diderot, Brecht, Eisenstein', deal with issues relating to the cinematic 'still' in which Barthes writes suggestively of fundamental distinctions to be made between film and photography.

reason that film is able to convince the viewer of the actual presence of something is because of its ability to render movement. The reasons for this, according to Metz, are twofold. By presenting us with successive images of objects moving within space, film lends them a greater corporeality and they therefore appear to us as more 'real' then in the photograph. Moreover, the distinction between the material properties of an object and its representation – which are always evident in a photograph – 'dissolves on the threshold of motion'. This is because movement can never be represented: it is always actual movement and the viewer always sees it as being present.

Because movement is never material but is always visual, to reproduce its appearance is to duplicate its reality. In truth, one cannot even 'reproduce' a movement: one can only re-produce it in a second production belonging to the same order of reality, for the spectator, as the first. It is not sufficient to say that film is more 'living', more 'animated' than still photography, or even that filmed objects are more 'materialised'. In the cinema the impression of reality is also the reality of impression, the real presence of motion.[5]

The distinctions between film and photography thus appear as stark and absolute: on the one hand we have movement that not only is present but also lends to the image a 'presence', and, on the other hand, we have a moment frozen in time and an immobility that is lodged within an ever-receding past that can only testify to an absence. It would seem foolish to argue against this perspective (although I will later have cause to question its rigidity). Indeed, some of Claerbout's video installations would appear to juxtapose film and photography precisely with attention to these distinctions. In addition to *Vietnam, 1967, near Duc Pho* , works such as *Kindergarten Antonio Sant'Elia, 1932* and *Ruurlo, Bocurloscheweg, 1910* , all make use of archival photographs in which an historical past is summoned up not only through the image itself but also through the title of the work. It would be difficult to deny that these works are not permeated by the sense of loss that the photograph inevitably brings in its wake and are suffused to some extent by a sense of melancholia. Whilst in one work an image taken from a postcard made in the early twentieth century presents a rural landscape that is itself lodged in the past, recalling as it does a time before the onset of modernity, the other, a scene of a group of children in the playground of a nursery school, evokes a sense of innocence made all the more poignant by our knowledge of events yet to come. Both, it would seem, lend themselves to a reading in the light of Barthes' formulation of the particular temporal character of the photograph that he draws from looking at the portrait of a young man awaiting execution: 'I read at the same time: *This will be and this has been;* I observe an anterior future of which death is at stake... *I shudder over a catastrophe that has already occurred.'*[6]

Barthes' sporadic writings on photography always struggled to find a suitable way of linguistically expressing the intractable nature of the photograph's temporality, whether through terms of what he described as 'an illogical conjuncture of *here-now* and the *there-then*' or in the paradoxical, grammatical notion of an 'anterior future'. Ultimately, however, the difficulties that gave rise to such terminological ambiguity would be surrendered, by many who have followed Barthes, to an overriding sense and interpretation of the photograph as bound to an instantaneous moment in time that inevitably and inexorably recedes into the past. Yet if the works of David Claerbout might seem at first to lend weight to such an understanding of the photograph, they must, I think, be read – at the very least – as bringing it into question.

An 'illogical conjuncture of *here-now* and the *there-then*' might be a suitable way to begin describing a work such as *Vietnam, 1967, near Duc Pho* with its visible intersection of filmic and photographic temporalities: with the appearance of motion in the large oak tree or the small saplings blown by the wind amidst the encompassing stillness of the image in *Ruurlo, Bocurloscheweg, 1910* and *Kindergarten Antonio Sant'Elia, 1932*. However, the works themselves undo any simple dichotomies between the filmic and the photographic, between present and past, between movement and stasis. The physical and imaginary homogeneity of both sides of the equation unravels within a single, undifferentiated and unified space that each literally, simultaneously and inextricably, occupy. Yet whilst this imperceptible interweaving of the photographic and the filmic within the unified surface of the image takes place we cannot say that each forfeits its specific identity. The work, we might say, would seem to belong to both film and photography but, then again, it would appear to be neither strictly a film nor simply a photograph.

As a means of approaching what might be involved in this intimate juxtaposition of film and photography, of movement and stillness, we can turn to Raymond Bellour's analysis of what happens when we are confronted by the occurrence of the image of the photograph in certain examples of classical narrative cinema. Whilst Bellour grants that photographs represented as objects

5 Christian Metz, *Film Language: A Semiotics of the Cinema*,
  Oxford University Press, 1974, p. 9.

6 Roland Barthes, *Camera Lucida: Reflections on Photography*,
  Hill and Wang, New York, 1980, p. 96.

within a film are used to advance a story and that they are therefore caught up in the time of an unfolding narrative, their appearance nonetheless is problematic for the film's diegesis. In the examples he gives, the photograph is used as an emblematic motif around which the plot of the film might hinge (often at points in the narrative in which the passage of time is being marked through acts of remembrance), yet at precisely this moment the temporal flow of the film is arrested, its narrative momentum suspended albeit briefly. At this point at which 'the film seems to freeze, to suspend itself', the viewer is made aware of two kinds of temporality: that which belongs to the film and the intrinsic forward movement of the narrative, and that which is the time of viewing the film and which carries the phenomenological force of the here and now. Thus paradoxically it is the photograph caught on film that directs our attention to the present – even as it functions within the narrative of the film in accordance with its predominant cultural forms to symbolize the past.

The presence of the photograph, diverse, diffuse, ambiguous, thus has the effect of uncoupling the spectator from the image, even if only slightly, even if only by virtue of the extra fascination it holds. It pulls the spectator out of this imprecise, yet pregnant force: the ordinary imaginary of the cinema....The photo thus becomes a stop within a stop, a freeze-frame within a freeze-frame; between it and the film from which it emerges, two kinds of time blend together, always and inextricable, but without becoming confused. [7]

Extending this argument, Garrett Stewart notes that Bellour's analysis is constrained by the cinematic phenomena he uses.[8] The placing of a photograph as an identifiable object within the illusory space of the film, even where that object may be co-extensive with the screen frame, whilst not without ramifications for film's narrative spatio-temporal diegesis, ultimately leaves it in place. What Stewart contrasts with this phenomenon of an image-within-an-image is the instance of the true freeze-frame, where 'the difference in question is between imaged motionlessness and the 'motionless' image.' It is only in the case of the latter, when the elemental unit of film itself – a single photogram – is isolated and then multiplied and projected that the critical interrogation of 'the ordinary imaginary of the cinema' is truly engaged. Since the freeze frame is actual stasis, and not merely its representation, its appearance on the screen is

a moment of hiatus, not only in the temporal momentum of the film's narrative but also, potentially, in the illusion of reality to which it is bound. The freeze-frame, argues Stewart, allows the possibility of cinematic reflexivity; although interestingly this is achieved through something that might be deemed not to belong to the medium of film and that may take us outside of the film. With the freeze-frame the film images itself: 'The film has become, so to speak, transparent to itself, but only in the moment, and at the price, of its cancelled succession, its negation as a moving picture.'[9]

It is necessary here to draw together the notion of the effects of the stilling of the moving image in the example of the freeze-frame – theorized by Garrett Stewart as a potential moment of filmic reflexivity – with the idea of the film's 'presentness'. The idea that film reveals to us actions or events that we take to be immediately present has been, as I noted earlier, a founding principle in discussions of the medium. Yet what does it mean when it is claimed, as it was by Robbe-Grillet, that 'the essential characteristic of the [film] image is its presentness', and that 'by its very nature what we see on the screen is in the act of happening, we are given the gesture itself, not an account of it'? Obviously, such a claim does not mean that we cannot comprehend or recognize distinctions between 'past' and 'present' or indeed 'future' as these are signified within the codes and conventions of narrative film. To this extent narrative film shares with literature (albeit in a more restricted way) the ability to articulate different tenses. We need, therefore, to distinguish between 'presentness', as in the sense of the present tense, and that which we experience as being present in real-life time. Whereas the present tense is a property of (filmic) language, the latter belongs to our encounter with the perceptual phenomena of the film's presentation in the here and now. It is, of course, in the foregrounding of an experiential 'here and now', in the convergence of real time with screen time, that film is able to achieve a 'presence' that is, in Stewart's terms, 'reflexive'.

Two points interest me here. Firstly, reflexivity. The notion of reflexivity, whether one is concerned with film or photography or painting or whatever, has been central to theories of medium specificity. Indeed, we can observe that it is only through reflexivity – or as Clement Greenberg called it a process of 'self criticism' – that it has been thought possible to identify those properties and

7 Raymond Bellour 'The Pensive Spectator', *Wide Angle, Vol. 9, no. 1*, 1987, p. 10.

8 See Garrett Stewart, ' Photo-gravure: Death, Photography and Film Narrative', *Wide Angle, Vol. 9, no. 6*, 1987, pp. 11-40. Stewart expanded the issues first raised in this essay in his later book *Between Film and Screen: Modernism's Photo Synthesis*, University of Chicago Press, 1999.

9 See Stewart, ' *Photo-gravure: Death, Photography and Film Narrative*', p. 19.

...haracteristics that are peculiar and unique to it, in other words, to define its essence'. Yet, it would seem from Stewart's example of the freeze-frame that reflexivity in film is best, or perhaps only, possible through the deployment of a device that does not 'belong' to film, one that runs counter to common assumptions about the medium and the centrality of movement to it. Stasis or virtual stasis in various guises, ranging from the lack of movement of the camera to the fixity of objects placed before it, has always been regarded as uncinematic. But the sudden appearance of the freeze frame is, according to Stewart, such a fundamental rupture in the filmic text, that it creates a kind of acinema. I am tempted to call such an acinematic form photography.

Secondly, at this moment of reflexivity, a point where the film folds back upon itself, it paradoxically surrenders its autonomy. Precisely when we might expect a kind of closure the film reveals – we could say *discloses* – itself. It is being watched. In its suspension of the momentum of the narrative, the stilled image flows out into the here and now of the time of viewing allowing for the possibility of what Bellour calls 'the pensive spectator'.

Neither Bellour's nor Stewart's line of thought carries as much critical edge if transposed from the domain of narrative cinema to that of contemporary art practice, where 'reflexivity' has been an avant-garde gambit – particularly as regards the deconstuction of the medium of film – for some time now. Yet I think they offer useful insights as to what might be involved in the intimate juxtaposition of the moving and still image in the work of David Claerbout. The main point that I want to develop here is that his work stages a radical conjuncture of photography and film through which each is exposed to the other, each is made open in terms of a reading through the other. An entry point to such an analysis is possibly through a consideration of the time of, and within, the image.

In the works of Claerbout that I have already mentioned the passage of time is one gauged by subtle movements in natural phenomena, such as the shadows of clouds cast on a hillside or the swaying of the branches and leaves of a tree blown in the wind. However, the actual movement we observe is minimal: not much 'happens'. Whatever movement occurs is endlessly repeated and since the transition point within the cycle or repetition is imperceptible, the result is an experience for the viewer of an unbounded duration. The evident absence of any transformation from one state to another leaves the impression of time stood still. If not actual stasis, the effect comes close to it. If film, in this instance, drifts towards the photographic, a movement in the opposite direction seems also to be possible. To explore this further we can turn to Claerbout's photographic work.

Alongside his large-scale video installations, Claerbout has continually made still photographic work. Most of this has taken the form of series of moderately large lightbox transparencies. Views of Venice or landscape scenes shot in conditions of twilight at either dawn or dusk, required lengthy exposure times even after which the image was still barely registered on the light sensitized surface of the photographic film. As a result, even when installed in conditions of total darkness, the image contained within the illuminated photographic transparency is imperceptible to the viewer on first entering the space. Only after a considerable time – during which the viewer's eyes adjust to the negligible levels of illumination – does the image become slowly visible. The viewer's experience of these works is thus analogous to the actual process of manufacturing a photographic print in a darkroom, where the 'developing' image only slowly emerges over a period of time during which more of its details are seen. Temporal duration is thus an integral component of these works, the time of their production mirroring the time of their reception. Curiously, Claerbout's use of pre-digital optical and chemical technologies in his still photographic work resuscitates a qualitative feature of the medium in its infancy. Walter Benjamin once noted that part of the fascination of some of the earliest photographic portraits lay with their particular relationship to the passage of time due to the low light sensitivity of photographic plates that required prolonged exposures. 'The procedure itself', he noted, 'caused the subject to focus his life in the moment rather than hurrying past it; during the considerable period of the exposure, the subject as it were grew into the picture, in the sharpest contrast with appearances in the snapshot...'.[10] Whilst later technical developments enabled the instantaneity of the photograph, violently severing the individual moment from the passage of time, in these early images Benjamin perceived time as leaching out into the image through a process of duration.

Contrary to the arguments that photography leads to the atomization and fragmentation of our sense of time, rendering reality as a collection of isolated and discreet moments, Claerbout's work reinvests the photographic image with time, lending to it an objective durational presence. And whilst this is something that is more clearly evident in the photographic works, it is also something that helps to explain the effect of the video installations. Within the differentiated

10 Walter Benjamin, 'A Short History of Photography', trans. Stanley Mitchell, *Screen*, 13, 1972, pp. 5 – 27.

surface of these images on which the static and moving image simultaneously coexist there may not be any actual convergence of the photographic and the filmic, but there is nonetheless an exchange that takes place between them. It is as if the parts of the image that remain still steal something from those that move, giving credence to Claerbout's desire to 'unfreeze the photograph'. This is a material and not merely a mental incidence.

It can hardly have escaped notice that the discussion of the still photograph in Claerbout's work has so far failed to draw explicit attention to the fact that none of these images belong to the most common physical form that the photograph has taken. None of them are made to be seen as photographic prints, as images transferred onto a piece of paper, and their appearance in this publication in such a form as documentation belies a fundamental aspect of the viewer's direct experience of them.

It has often been argued that the literal and palpable existence of the photograph as an actual physical object serves to underline a particular modality of vision that is marked by photography's sense of 'possession' of the material object that it pictures. The 'realism' of photography, and the evidential testimony to the existence of things, converges with the existence of the photograph as a thing in itself. Moreover there is also a sense in which photography's atomization of time, its freezing of a singular moment isolated and abstracted from the temporal flow, finds concrete form in a thing that can be held in the hand, literally grasped. Thus it could be argued that Barthes' influential dualistic model of a phenomenology of the photography, split between the 'here and now' and the 'there and then', is premised upon a single, if the most common, physical manifestation of the photograph. My argument here is that the act of continually shuffling between the dichotomies of absence and presence, past and present, proximity and distance, begins and ends with the fact of the palpable existence of the photographic print itself. As Philippe Dubois has noted:

This separation within the representation is what actually informs the effect of looking at a photograph, inducing perpetual movement on the part of the spectator-subject: we pass continually from the object's here-and-now to its elsewhere-in-the-past when looking at the image....The photograph acts as an instrument of travel in time and memory. To see something that existed, somewhere, sometime, something

that is much more present in our imagination now that we know it has actually disappeared – to see it and not be able to touch, pick up, or manipulate it – is to be frustrated by a metonymic substitute for the thing that is gone forever, now a simple trace on a piece of paper instead of a single palpable memory. The frustration is all the stronger for the indexical substitute signifies the absence of the referent, offering itself qua representation, as a concrete object endowed with real, physical substance.[11]

If this is the case, what is the effect of those material and objective forms that the photograph can take that would seem to go some way to 'dematerializing' the photographic image? A photographic transparency – whether enlarged and illuminated from behind (as with Claerbout's lightboxes) or projected onto a screen – is stripped of the palpable material support of the image that defines the phenomonological status of the photographic print. We might argue that as a consequence of this the projected photographic image also has a very different relationship to time. If the tactile and physical existence of the photographic print 'functions to fix a *being-that-has been* (a presence in the present that is always past)', could it be that the projected still photograph 'functions as a *coming into being* (a presence always presently constituting itself)'?[12] The projected image is always, as it were, in a continual process of being reconstituted: dependent upon the continuous supply of artificial illumination it is always 'live'. We might say that our experience of the projected image's existence in time – as taking time – is more akin to watching a film than looking at a photographic print. Certainly it shares with the film the same conditions of viewing: the projection of a luminous image in a darkened space. Such forms of convergence might suggest that the distinction between the photographic and filmic is less secure than is usually assumed.

Others, however, would contend that the distinction between the projected photograph and film has been and remains absolute. Even when we are dealing with the case of the freeze-frame of a film and a projected still photograph (which might be perceptually indistinguishable), if 'you know that what you are watching is a film, even a film of what appears to be a photograph, it is always justifiable to expect that the image *might* move.'[13] Certainly there is something to this. The knowledge that what one is watching is a film predisposes us to anticipate the possibility of movement and expect it, at some time, to occur. This

11 Philippe Dubois, 'Photography Mise-en-Film: Autobiographical (Hi)stories and Psychic Apparatuses, trans. Lynne Kirby, in Patrice Pedro (ed.) *Fugitive Images: from photography to video*, Indiana University Press, 1995,

12 The phraseology here (emphasis added) is taken from Vivian Sobchack 'The Scene of the Screen: Envisioning Cinematic and Electronic Presence', in Hans Ulrich Gumbrecht and K. Ludwig Pfeiffer (eds.) *Materialities*

13 Noel Carroll, 'Towards an Ontology of the Moving Image', in Cynthia A. Freeland and Thomas E. Wartenburg (eds.) *Philosophy and Film*, Routledge, 1995, p. 73.

is what happens, of course, in Chris Marker's *La Jetée*. It also explains the tension that accompanies David Claerbout's video projection *Four Persons Standing* where our expectation is not met and our anticipation is thwarted since movement never occurs. Yet isn't this argument, traceable as it is to the idea of fundamental distinctions that can be made between mediums on the basis of their differing technology's, unsustainable in the face of what electronic and digital technologies are capable of? And have not these new technologies in erasing the empirical boundaries between the old technologies of film and photography, simultaneously undermined any obvious distinction that we might wish to make between the moving and the still image?

The progression of my argument has led to questions that would seem to run counter to my earlier assertion that the concept of the medium remains important and useful. Yet, to repeat myself, mediums are technologies but they are never reducible to technology. A medium is always constituted within a particular social and discursive matrix. As a technology that is always socially and discursively positioned, a medium is an historical phenomenon. And if photography and film are not immutable entities it is not only because of any transformations in their technological foundations but also because what they 'mean' is always historically fluid. However, it seems possible that, whilst technological developments have certainly eroded any simple distinctions between the moving and still image, the categories of 'photography' and 'film' remain the only ways in which we can still talk about such things. The concept of the medium is indispensable, it seems, even in 'the age of the post-medium condition'.

One final point. As I suggested earlier it is a logical consequence of the fact that a particular medium is defined in terms of its distinction from other mediums that it is 'unthinkable' in its own terms. The pursuit of a medium's essential properties by means of a kind of auto-reflexivity is an impossibility inasmuch as the medium is continually caught in a process of being defined by what it is not rather than (or, more precisely, simultaneously as) what it is. Therefore what is deemed as lying 'outside' of a particular medium will always be present and effective in defining what it is. When Greenberg wrote about how one defined the specificity of a medium, he saw this as a process whereby one discovered its 'limiting conditions'. Such a process was necessary in order to 'entrench' the medium 'more firmly in its area of competence'. Yet, perhaps, the more interesting and productive area (for artists and critics) has been at this limit point. An area of 'undecidability'. And maybe this is what the work of David Claerbout's faces us with, in the possibility of a photograph that unfolds in time (but is not a film) and a film that is stilled in time (but is not a photograph).

Previous page:
Ruurlo, Bocurloscheweg, 1910,
1997. Video Installation,
b/w, silent. Installation view
Sammlung Goetz,
Munich, 2001.

Opposite:
Venice Lightbox (Santa
Maria del Salute), 2000
110 x 150 x 20 cm.

Venice Lightbox (Ca d'Oro),
2000. 110 x 150 x 20 cm

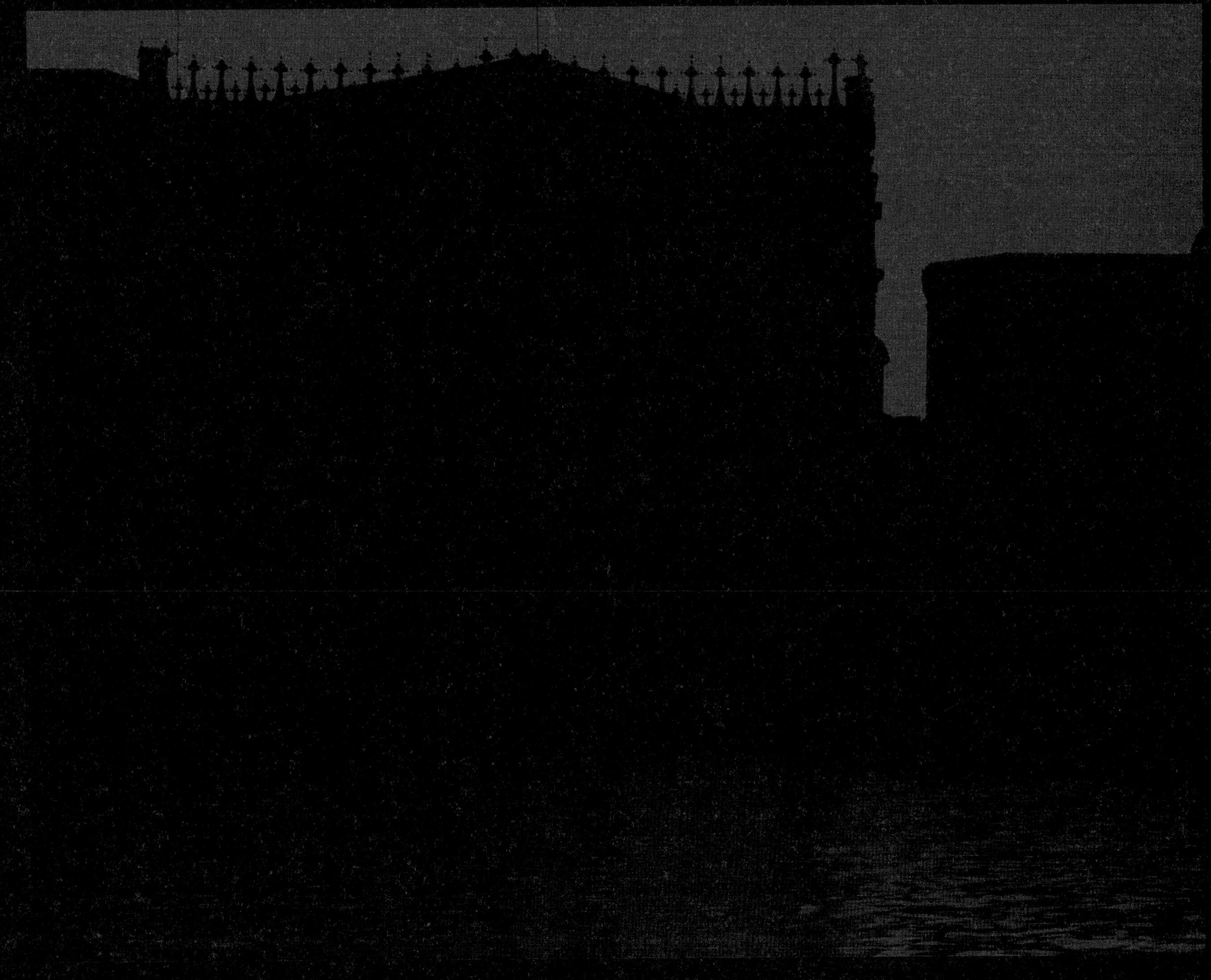

Venice Lightbox
(Isola San Giorgio), 2000.
110 x 150 x 20 cm

*Venice Lightbox
(Isola San Miguele)*, 2000.
110 x 150 x 20 cm.

Images, Mechanisms and Time

Gregory Currie

Photography is philosophically important for two reasons: its relation to time, and to objects. We can put these two things together and say: a photograph stands in a peculiar relation to an object at a time. It is commonly said that a photograph 'captures' an object at a time. There is something in this, but it raises other questions: Is this kind of capturing different from anything a painting or drawing can achieve? What about the use of photographs and photograph-like media in representing movement and change through time? To understand anything at all about this relation we have to start with what has always seemed the most basic but also the most problematic fact about photographs: their mechanicity.

The idea that photography is *mere* mechanical reproduction of appearances seems obviously wrong: too many actual photographs seem to transform their objects in aesthetic and other ways. Anyway, looking at a photograph of an object is not often mistaken for looking at the object itself. But there is surely something in the idea of mechanicity. The questions are what, and what are its consequences?

It helps to start with the idea of an accidental photograph. A photograph is something that can simply *happen*, as when the mechanism is accidentally set off. When that happens we may end up with an image – a representation – of something that no one planned to represent. True, the mechanism itself is a product of design, so there is intention somewhere along the line. But we have here already a substantial difference between photography and painting; pots of paint may be manufactured, but if a cyclone blows the paint into a shape that happens to look like Durham Cathedral, we don't have a representation of the cathedral, but merely a pattern that resembles one. There are, in this sense, no accidental paintings *of* things. There can be accidents *in* painting; the painter paints one thing thinking it is another. There is a sense, in that case, in which she painted something other than what she intended to paint. But there is another sense in which she painted exactly what she wanted to paint. She wanted to paint *that* Cathedral – the one directly in front of her – and that is what she painted, even if she is mistaken about which cathedral it is.

Retrospection, 2000.
Video Installation, b/w, silent.

There are, or seem to be, other differences of a related kind between painting and photography. A photograph, accidental or deliberate, records only what is there, what exists – and indeed only what exists at a certain place and time. A photograph is always of just that thing which stands in a certain relation to the photograph itself. That relation is what philosophers call 'causal'; a photograph is of the thing that was in front of the lens, and which transmitted light into the lens. And a photograph of a man dressed as Jesus is a photograph of that man and not of Jesus. But there are pictures 'of' all sorts of things that don't exist and which an audience will typically not assume exists: we can paint people who died centuries ago, events which never happened and people from myth and legend who never existed. A good objection here would be to say that there cannot really be a picture of something that does not exist, for then what is it a picture of? The only answer that makes sense is 'nothing'. The objection is good, and that is why I put 'of' in scare quotes earlier. But then the point can be made in a different way. Painting is capable of something – we unreflectively call it 'picturing nonexistent things', but it is hard to say precisely what that is – that photography is not capable of.[1]

The contrasting relationships between photography and painting are encapsulated in the relations between two films. The first is *Blow Up*, by Michelangelo Antonioni. Here a photograph is taken of a scene, and the photographer comes to suspect that something is captured on the film that he had no knowledge of at the time the photograph was taken. Enlarging the image shows that this is indeed the case; he sees that the photograph captures a dead body under a hedge. Obviously this story would not work for painting: a painter cannot, unknowingly, paint a dead body under a hedge in such a way that the shape of the body would become clear by enlarging the image. As I have said, mistakes are possible in paintings and drawings, and artists can be mistaken about the significance of what they paint and draw – a situation exploited in Peter Greenaway's film *The Draftsman's Contract* – but the range of possible mistakes here is different from those available in photography.

These are some aspects, or consequences, of the mechanicity of photography. But what exactly is the mechanicity of photographs? Any workable account of mechanicity must accommodate the fact that (most) photographs are not accidents, and that indeed great skill and artistry can be expressed through the medium. The best account anyone has offered is, I think, that of the philosopher Kendall Walton, who argues that photographs are mechanical in so far as they depend on what is there in front of the camera, and do not depend on what the photographer thinks is there. If a painter is having an hallucination, and thinks he sees an elephant in front of him, an elephant is what he will paint if he chooses to represent the scene. But an hallucinating photographer will not photograph an elephant if there is, in fact, no elephant there.

Walton goes on to make a further claim that some find startling: that photographs are, as he puts it, *transparent*: when we see a photograph of an egg, we see – literally see – the egg itself. Of course this does not mean that the egg is present, or that touching the photograph is touching the egg, or that you are seeing the egg in the way you would be if the egg were there in front of you. But we already recognise different ways of seeing *things*. When I see stars through a telescope I certainly cannot touch them and indeed the light from them took so long to get here that they may actually have ceased to exist by the time I am seeing them. Photography, says Walton, is a new way of seeing things. Painting is not, on the other hand, a way of seeing things. We don't see the egg when we see a painting of one. And the reason for that is to be found in the way that seeing photographs of things is like seeing things in the ordinary immediate way, but seeing things in paintings isn't.[3] Photography and direct perception are independent of intention in the sense described above, but painting isn't. But note: the idea that photography is mechanical is distinct from the idea that it is transparent. You can accept the first of these ideas without accepting the second.

Returning to the idea of capturing an object in time, what I have said about the photograph's mechanicity suggests that the capturing here is distinctive in that it is independent of intention: what the photograph presents is the object as it was at that time – not how I thought it was. And if Walton is right to say that photography is transparent, the capturing is more than just a matter of representation: the photograph presents the object to us. But it presents it, as we shall see, in a very distinctive way.

An important issue about photography and time arises when we consider, not still photography but the moving images of cinema. This argument applies

1 This point was recognised very early in the history of photography, though generally expressed in other ways. Talbot added a note to his book of photographs of 1844 saying that they were made "by the agency of light alone". And this thought has co-existed with the apparently contrary

1864: "My aspirations are to ennoble photography and to secure for it the character and uses of High Art". Later we shall see how far these ambitions are consistent.

2 See Kendall Walton, 'Transparent pictures', *Critical Inquiry* 11,

3 Walton's thesis is criticised in a number of places. See eg Gregory Currie, *Image and Mind*, Cambridge University Press, 1995.

also, in less obvious ways, to video, which I will discuss in a moment, but it is easiest to state the problem in terms of photography and cinematography.

Suppose we grant that photographs are transparent: that when we see a photograph we see – literally see – the thing it is a photograph of. Now even someone who accepts this view will agree that, in the case of an ordinary photograph, we do not see movement. We see the object, but we do not see any movement of the object, even if the object was in fact moving at the time that the photograph was taken. There is nothing odd about that. When we see something, we do not see every aspect of it, and sometimes when we see objects, do not see their movement. The stars are moving very quickly relative to us but we do not see their movement when we casually look at them.

Cinematography is a medium that depends on photography, inasmuch as cinema involves the projection of a succession of static photographic images on a screen. By projecting these images in very quick succession (normally at a rate of 24 frames per second) we are able to create a moving image, or at least the impression of movement. But, so the argument goes, this impression of movement is an illusion. Out of this argument is born the idea that the basic mechanism of cinema is based on illusion, and this has had profound consequences for thinking about cinema. It has, for example, encouraged the view that cinema is an illusory medium in other ways, in that it creates in the viewer a regression to an infantile state of passivity in which the screen becomes a substitute for the real world, with the viewer temporarily convinced that what he or she is watching is real.[4] But my concern here is with the argument about time and movement just presented, rather than with these larger issues about cinema ideology. Is it right to say that the movement we see on the screen is illusory?[5]

Remember what the argument is supposed to be: a cinematic image is constructed from the projection of a succession of still photographs; these images do not, individually, allow us to see movement; therefore, they do not collectively allow us to see movement.

But this argument is hopeless. There are very many cases where a bunch of things has some feature not had by any of the things individually. A crowd may be large in a sense in which none of its individual members is. Anyway, the argument proves too much; if it proves that we do not really see motion on the screen it also proves that we do not seem to see motion on the screen – but everyone agrees that we do at least seem to see motion. Recall, the argument was that since there is no motion seen in individual photographs, there is no real motion seen in a sequence of them. But there is also no appearance of motion in any individual photograph. So, by the same reasoning, we should conclude that there is no appearance of motion on the cinema screen.

Someone might try to put the argument in a different way: if we look at the film strip itself, instead of looking at the projected image, we shall not see any motion in the objects there represented; we see only a succession of still images. Hence, when we seem to see motion on the screen, that must be an illusion. This argument applies as well to the case of video, because we can also examine the video tape and find no motion on its surface; there is simply a complex pattern of magnetization across its surface.

Unfortunately this version of the argument proves that we never hear sounds when we listen to a recording. After all, take the CD out of the player and examine it most minutely. Where is the sound? You will not hear any, however close to your ear you place the CD. To hear the sound, you have to place the CD in a machine and to operate it in the right manner. When you do so, you do actually hear a sound. You are not subject to an illusion that you are hearing sound. In fact most people would be happy to agree that what you hear is really the instrument or voice that was recorded. We really do hear Pavarotti when we listen to a recording of him. The idea that all this is an illusion is not worth considering.

It is also difficult to see how one could combine the view that we really see people when we see their photographs with the view that we do not really see their movements when we watch them on film. For if we do not see their movements, then how is it that we see them at all? Do we see them, but not see them moving? Surely, if we see them at all, we see them moving. Once again, the idea that we see movie actors on screen, but actually see them stationary when we think we see them moving is not worth considering.

If my reasoning is right here, then film and video are genuinely media in which movement is presented, as is change of other kinds: on film we can see things change colour or shape. This brings us to an important point. Film and

4 This approach to cinema, which depends heavily on ideas from a version of Freudian psychology, has been criticised by scholars such as Noel Carroll, whose book *Mystifying Movies* (New York, 1990) is a refreshing antidote to the flat-footed mixture of Freud, Marx and semiotic ideas which has done so much damage to film theory. See also the collection of critical essays in David Bordwell and Noel Carroll (eds) *Post-Theory*, University of Wisconsin Press, 1996.

5 Some aspects of the argument below are developed in more detail in my *Image and Mind*.

video are media of time, because they present to us things that are happening in time, and do so by using time itself. Let me explain this last idea.

It is possible to use photography in such a way that change is represented, without using time in the way that film and video use time. I might lay out before you a series of still photographs; by looking at them, you can see the successive states of an object as it moves. Muybridge's photographs of humans and animals in motion did that, and settled old debates about how these things move. (Do horses ever have all their feet of the ground when they gallop? Muybridge settled this question.) But a sequence of still photographs laid out in this way does not represent a temporal medium or a temporal art. When photographs are laid out in this way we are free to look at them as we like, and there is no required amount of time that you have to spend looking at each one, or between each act of looking, in order to get the information from them concerning movement.

Film on the other hand is, in a serious and deep sense, a temporal art, because it not only represents time, it uses time to represent time. Standardly in film, the time it takes for us to see a continuous action is just the same as the time it takes for the action to take place. Other media represent time; time is represented in the novel, for example, in the sense that what is represented is things happening in time, where the reader often has, on the basis of reading, a good idea about how long they took. The author can simply *tell you* how long that event took. So in a sense, the novel is an art of time. It is an art form that represents time. But it does not use time to represent time, in the way that cinema does. The standard mode of presentation for film is for the filmic presentation to last just the same amount of time as the event does. Of course a film can, wholly or in part, be in slow motion, or speeded up; the point is that film has the *capacity* to represent a given interval of time by means of that very interval of time. And that capacity is, as a matter of fact, widely exploited by film-makers for good reason: it provides the audience with information about the durations of events without their having to make inferences. The audience simply experiences that very duration.

Of course in film there is the possibility of cutting, and so this creates the possibility that events are represented in truncated form. In the old montage style of Soviet Cinema this was sometimes taken to extreme, with many cuts and very short intervals between the cuts. This allows for the manipulation of the audience's sense of the duration of a represented event, as with the clearing of the steps at Odessa by the soldiers in *The Battleship Potemkin,* which takes much more time on the film than the event would have taken in real time. Still, the point

remains that a film has to consist of conjoined shots, and what has been said above concerning the representation of time by time holds for any given shot.

This is not merely a question about the logic of cinematic presentation; it has important aesthetic and expressive implications. One dimension of freedom in film is the extent to which the maker uses the temporal possibilities of the medium. However, there is a line of argument we need to consider which says this: since photography is transparent – since, in other words, the photograph allows us to see the thing it is a photograph of, photography (and, by implication, film and video) have no aesthetic possibilities at all. They are simply ways we can present things, as putting a frame around an object would be. Transparency means that what is interesting about the photograph is what it is of, and not it itself. Since photographs present objects rather than representing them, they have no status as representational art, and indeed no status as art at all.

That roughly speaking is the argument of Roger Scruton.[6] What should we make of it? One response to this would be to deny that photographs are transparent, something I have not so far tried to do. As a matter of fact, I don't myself believe that photographs are transparent. But this is not an easy debate to settle. I would prefer to respond to the 'photographs have no aesthetic' claim without making everything depend on the denial of transparency. And I think this can be done. Here I draw on an argument recently given by Don Lopes.[7]

Lopes agrees with those who say that photographs are transparent. He asks: If we see objects when we see photographs of them, how can a photograph engage any aesthetic interest not engaged just by looking at the object itself? His answer is that we need to distinguish between two kinds of seeing (both of which are, genuinely, kinds of seeing). There is seeing things directly, and there is seeing things through photographs (there are other kinds, like seeing things in mirrors, but they are not relevant here). The aesthetic interest of a photograph is, he agrees, limited to the interest of the object seen through the photograph; but this is not the same as the interest of the object seen directly. In other words, the fact that photographs are transparent does not mean that they are aesthetically irrelevant; it means that their aesthetic relevance is as ways of seeing objects. And that means that they can have plenty of aesthetic interest. Here time once again becomes important. One of the distinctive things about seeing things

6 See R. Scruton, 'Photography and Representation', in *The Aesthetic Understanding.* London: Methuen, 1983.

7 See D. McIver Lopes, 'The Aesthetics of Photographic Transparency', *Mind 112,* 2003.

through photographs is that we see them 'frozen in time', which is not how we see them when we see them directly. This is particularly obvious when we consider an object that is moving or otherwise changing at the time the photograph is taken, but it can be of aesthetic interest even when the object was not moving at that time. There is a difference between watching an object which happens to remain still over the time you watch it, and watching, for an equally long period, a photograph of that object. In these two situations one is, so to speak, in quite distinct worlds of possibility; when one looks at an object over time in the ordinary way there is a possibility of various kinds of change to the object, if only of position. When one looks at a photograph of an object, the only possibility for change lies with the photograph itself as a physical object.

Someone might insist that this is not relevant, because what makes an aesthetic difference is some actual difference between things and not a merely possible one. But there is ample reason to think that this view is wrong. Consider two pieces of recorded music that sound exactly the same. Might there be any aesthetic difference between them? Suppose one is a recording of a piano played in the ordinary way, and the other a recording of electronically generated sound that can't be distinguished from a piano. Knowing this, our aesthetic responses to these two things would be different, because we would know that each involved a different structure of possibilities. Things can go wrong when playing the piano that can't go wrong when generating sound electronically (perhaps things can go wrong with the latter, but they are different things). The old idea that aesthetic responses are responses to 'mere appearances' is surely wrong.[8]

In addition to all this, there is simply the interest that can be generated by the fact that the object was photographed at a particular time, and what we are seeing now – when looking at the photograph – is something we could not possibly see if we were looking directly at the object. Looking directly at the object over a period of, say, five minutes, I see a certain stage in the life of the object. I see the object as it exists during that period. Nothing may happen to the object during that period, but still, something could happen to it. But if I spend five minutes looking at the photograph of the object I am seeing something quite different (though it might not look very different); I am seeing, for five minutes, the object as it was at an instant. As before, the structure of possibilities implicit in these two experiences is quite different.

All this concerns what is sometimes called an 'ideal' photograph, and we know that photography and – even more obviously – digital technology are media within which it is possible to intervene in such a way that one gains increased intentional control. Does this vitiate the points I have been making? I think not. The idea of mechanicity in photography and other forms of image making remains a potent aesthetic force, even in situations where the image is highly manipulated. For in these situations one has a sense of the artist working against the grain of the medium. Much earlier I said that photography has an aspect which is independent of the maker's intention: a photographer may intend to depict a monster in the Loch, but if what is in front of the lens is simply a bit of drift wood, that is what gets depicted. The default position for photography and like media is the representation of what is there, even though the default can be overcome. In painting and drawing the situation is quite different, because the standard uses of these media are ones that require detailed intentional control at every stage. What is perhaps comparable within the domain of painting and drawing to image manipulation in photography and digital technology is the deliberate (but partial) giving up of intentional control we are familiar with from the work of painters like Jackson Pollock.

No medium imposes absolute boundaries on what can be done, and there are no laws that forbid the mixing or conjoining of media. What starts life as a photograph may end up indistinguishable from a painting. One thing photography shows us is that how we arrive at the image is as interesting and important as the image itself. If painting and mechanistic modes of image making meet in the middle here, it remains an aesthetically important fact that they are arriving from opposite directions.

8 See my An Ontology of Art, London, 1989.

The Stack, 2002.
Video Installation, colour,
silent. Installation view at the
Kunstverein Hannover, 2002.

Acknowledgements

First Published in 2004 by
Photoworks
The Depot
100 North Road
Brighton
England BN1 1YE
t: +44 (0)1273 607500
e: info@photoworksuk.org
www.photoworksuk.org

Distributed by
Cornerhouse Publications
70 Oxford Street
Manchester
England M1 5NH.
t: +44 (0)161 200 1503
e: publications@cornerhouse.org
www.cornerhouse.org/publications

British Library Cataloguing-In-Publication Data. A catalogue
record for this book is available from the British Library.

ISBN 1-903796-12-1

Edited by David Green
Design by LOUP
Printed by Dexter Graphics

This book is published to coincide with an exhibition of the work of David
Claerbout at the Herbert Read Gallery, Canterbury held from 19 April to 8 May 2004.
The exhibition, curated with the assistance of Joanna Lowry, was made possible
by the generous support of Arts Council England South East. Special thanks
for their help with the organisation of the exhibition go to Martin Clark and
Manuel Miseur.

This book would not have been possible without the assistance of a number
of institutions and individuals. The Arts and Humanities Research Board and
the Centre for Research Development, Faculty of Arts and Architecture at the
University of Brighton funded my research towards this publication. Financial
assistance towards the publication itself was given by Arts Council England
South East, the University of Brighton and Kent Institute of Art and Design.
Amongst those individuals who have generously given their time or support
special thanks should go to Tse-Ling Uh of Hauser & Wirth Zürich London,
Jonathan Woodham, Paddy Maguire, David Campany and David Brittain. I must
also thank David Chandler and all the staff at Photoworks for their help and for
giving me the opportunity to put this publication together.

I am grateful to my co-authors in this publication, Joanna Lowry and Gregory
Currie, in providing two stimulating essays that – in very different ways – place
David Claerbout's work in a theoretical context.

It goes without saying that the exhibition and this publication would not
have been possible without the generosity of David Claerbout himself. To him
I owe my gratitude for his enthusiasm for the project and for time spent
discussing the work and the issues it raises.

David Green
April 2004

photoWORKS

David Claerbout was born in Kortrijk, Belgium in 1969. He attended the National Hoger Institut voor schone Kunsten, Antwerpen (1992-95). He currently lives and works in Berlin and Brussels. His work has been in numerous group exhibitions worldwide and he has had major solo exhibitions at the Hannover Kunstverein (2002) and the Centro Galego de Arte Contemporánea, Santiago de Compostela (2003). He achieved widespread critical acclaim for his contribution to the second Berlin Biennale in 2001 and he has also collaborated with the DIA Center, New York in a project for the internet in 2000 (see www.diacenter.org/claerbout). In October of 2004 a major exhibition of his work will be installed at the Kunstbau at Lehnbachhaus in Munich. Public collections that have acquired his work to date include the Museum für Modern Kunst, Frankfurt; ARC Musée d'Art Moderne de Ville, Paris; Musée d'Art Contemporain, Strassbourg; FRAC Nord Pas de Calais; and SMAK, Ghent. He is represented by Hauser & Wirth Zürich London, Galerie Micheline Szwajcer, Antwerp and Galerie Johnen + Schöttle, Cologne.

Joanna Lowry is Reader in Visual Theory and Media Arts at Kent Institute of Art and Design. She is the author of essays on the work of Douglas Gordon (in *Performing the Body, Performing the Text*, ed A. Jones & A. Stephenson, Routledge, 1999), Joseph Beuys and Yves Klein (in *Sculpture and Photography: Envisioning the Third Dimension*, ed G. Johnson, Cambridge University Press) and numerous catalogue essays including Rineke Dijkstra (The Photographers' Gallery, 1998), Cindy Sherman (Hasselblad Award, Goteborg, 1999) and Ori Gersht in *Afterglow: Ori Gersht* (August Books/ Tel Aviv Museum, 2002). She has also been a regular contributor to *Creative Camera, Portfolio* and other photographic journals.

David Green is Senior Lecturer in the History and Theory of Contemporary Art at the University of Brighton. He is the co-editor of *History Painting Reassessed* (Manchester University Press, 2000) and has contributed essays to *Camerawork, Ten/8, Oxford Art Journal, Creative Camera, Portfolio* and *Contemporary Visual Arts*. He is the editor and contributor to *Where is the Photograph?*, (Photoforum/ Photoworks, 2003). A major essay on the work of the painter David Reed has recently been published in *Critical Perspectives on Contemporary Painting: Hybridity, Hegemony, Historicism* (ed. J Harris, Tate Gallery/Liverpool University Press, 2003).

Gregory Currie is currently Professor of Philosophy at the University of Nottingham. He has published numerous articles on philosophical aspects of photography and film, including contributions to the *Routledge Encyclopedia of Philosophy*. His books include *The Nature of Fiction* (Cambridge University Press, 1990), *Image and Mind: Film, Philosophy and Cognitive Science* (Cambridge University Press, 1995) and *Recreative Minds: Imagination in Philosophy and Psychology* (Oxford University Press, 2002). A book of essays, *Arts and Minds*, will appear later this year (Oxford University Press, 2004).